Compendium of the Catholic Catechism on Freemasonry:

A Compendium of Theological and Historical Treatment Against Freemasonry and its Appendant Masonic Bodies

Published by:
Saint Dominic's Media, Inc.
www.saintdominicsmedia.com

Printed in the United States of America

1 2 3 4 5 6 7 8 9 10

BISAC Categories:
RELIGION / Christian Church / History
RELIGION / Christian Church / Canon & Ecclesiastical Law
RELIGION / Christianity / Catechisms

ISBN-13: 979-8-9857040-3-7 (Paperback)

Preface

I composed *The Catholic Catechism on Freemasonry* in 2020 with the main aim of clarifying the Church's unchanging doctrine on Freemasonry since Pope Clement XII's 1738 Papal Bull *In Eminenti apostolatus specula* (The High Warning) and why all Catholics must adhere to and obey what the Church has dogmatically taught.

This booklet is a concise summary of its original work that shows the official and consistent teachings of the Popes and the magisterium of the Catholic Church on the prohibition of Freemasonry.

This booklet is a handy resource that quickly explains the Church's beliefs and teachings on how the faithful are harmed by joining Freemasonry and how Freemasonry and its related Masonic groups have conspired against the Church throughout history.

The principle reason why a Catholic cannot be a Freemason is because the Church, whom Christ Jesus has charged to pasture, feed, and protect His flock, has dogmatically obligated us not to for the wellbeing of our soul. Indeed, it is a far better portion to arrive at our judgment day being able to tell God that we only believed what His Church has taught than confessing that we obeyed the mere dictates of our human reasoning.

Table of Contents

Page Six

1738—Papal Bull In Eminenti apostolatus specula, Pope Clement XII

Page Twelve

1751—Encyclical *Providas Romanorum*, Pope Benedict XIV

Page Eighteen

1873—Encyclical *Etsi Multa*, Bl. Pope Pius IX

Page Twenty-Four

1884—1994, Several Encyclicals, Pope Leo XIII

Page Forty-Three

1917—1983, One Encyclical, Two Canon Laws

1738

Pope Clement XII (1730—1740)
In Eminenti apostolatus specula

Pope Clement XII's pontificate legacy was his Apostolic Constitution *In Eminenti apostolatus specula* (The High Watch), published on April 28, 1738. This constitution (issued as a 'Papal Bull') lays out the foundations and grounds of the Catholic Church's opposition to Freemasonry. It explains how Freemasonry conspires against the Church, threatens the faith, and prohibits Catholics from joining, supporting, or advancing it and any of its related organizations.

Freemasonry, as it was organized then, with craft lodges under the authority of Grand Lodges and granting degrees to candidates based on the philosophical application of trade secrets and operative practices of freestone masonry, was still a young movement in 1738 but had already established Grand Lodges in England, Ireland, Scotland, France, Spain, Sweden, and even three in the new colonies (Massachusetts, Pennsylvania, and South Carolina). This modest number of Grand Lodges does not include the hundreds of subordinate lodges scattered across Europe and North America that were loyal to them.

By 1738, not only had the constitutions of the Grand Lodge of England been made public, but also, there had been at least eight exposés written about Freemasonry, which had revealed the secrets of their initiation ceremonies.

In this Papal bull, Pope Clement XII declared that Freemasonry, no matter where it is found or what it is called, is incompatible with Catholicism, not because of how individual Freemasons or groups practice it, but because the principles of Freemasonry are opposed to

Christ and His Church.

The permanent conflict and incompatibility between Catholicism and Freemasonry is based on these two arguments against Freemasonry, according to *In Eminenti apostolatus specula*.

1. **Freemasonry comprises "men of any Religion or sect, satisfied with the appearance of natural virtue."**

That is, Freemasonry practices indifferentism; it subordinates each man's personal religion under shade of it being their 'personal opinion' in the secular hope of dissuading disagreement among its members, and so that Freemasonry might be the 'universal religion' and the "Center of Union, and the Means of conciliating true Friendship among Persons that must have remain'd at a perpetual Distance." (Anderson, James. *Constitutions of the Free-Masons. Containing the History. Charges. Regulations. &c. of that most Ancient and Right Worshipful Fraternity.* 1728. Article I).

Pope Clement's charge that these men were satisfied with the appearance of **"natural virtue"** points to the fact that Freemasonry teaches its adherents that they can be good and true men without the help of God's grace. To matriculate in Freemasonry, one needs to prove proficiency in the natural things of this world. For example, how to use a gavel in the operative sense and apply the speculative principles of the gavel to one's life.

On the contrary, the great hope of the Catholic is not to matriculate in the eyes of men but, instead, to be made holy by God by cooperating with God through His grace.

The Freemason wants to be good and faithful and stand upright on the square, but the Catholic desires to be a saint in Heaven. For this reason, the Catholic finds nothing in Freemasonry that might aid him, and, thereby, he finds it a complete waste of time and a distraction from his preserving on the narrow way.

2. Freemasons "are associated with one another in a union, according to their laws and the statutes laid down for them, by a strict and unbreakable bond which obliges them, both by an oath upon the Holy Bible and by a host of grave penalties, to an inviolable silence about all that they do in secret together."

Here, Clement XII notes the irreconcilability between Catholicism and Freemasonry regarding its laws and statutes. Since the Catholic Church has its own laws and statutes that she obliges her children to obey, a Catholic cannot obligate themselves to obey a different and distinct body of laws and statutes under the coercion of secrecy and grave penalties.

Having to choose between obeying the laws and precepts of the Church or those of another entity is not a position that Catholics should ever place themselves in. For example, it may be the case that a subordinate lodge may summon a member to a lodge meeting. However, on the same day of the summon, the Catholic might be required to attend a solemn feast day. This person has a choice; if they fail to appear at the lodge on the call of a summons, they may face expulsion from the Masonic order. However, they incur a grave sin if they fail to appear at the Holy Mass.

While there are many civil service jobs in which a Catholic might make an oath on the Bible, those duties should never conflict with their duties to God, neighbor, and self. Nor should they be exercised in secret, lest they stir up the appearance of scandal and bring disrepute upon one's Church, community, and household.

By the time Clement XII promulgated *In Eminenti apostolatus specula*, Freemasonry had been banned in the Netherlands, Sweden, and Geneva. It had also been suppressed and persecuted in parts of Spain, Portugal, France, and Italy. **". . . in several countries these societies have been forbidden by the civil authorities as being against the public security, and for some time past have appeared to be prudently eliminated."** Therefore, Pope Clement XII is not acting arbitrarily here, even though he has the right to exercise such care as the Shepherd of all Christians. Rather, he is signaling that there is a maturing sense of the faithful that Freemasonry is **"depraved and perverted."**

From *In Eminenti* till today, there has never been a change in the Church's prohibitions against Freemasonry, inasmuch as the remedy to cure those afflicted by this sin of grave matter has been made more readily available and accessible through a Catholic priest.

The immediate outcome of *In Eminenti apostolatus specula* was that the prohibitions against Freemasonry were enforced in all of the Papal States (also called the

Republic of Saint Peter) in Italy. In many Catholic countries, lodges were dissolved, and the Supreme Sacred Congregation of the Roman and Universal Inquisition appointed commissioners throughout Europe to investigate individuals who were reportedly to have ties to Freemasonry. Some of these individuals were cleared of all charges against them. In contrast, others were excommunicated, tortured, imprisoned, banished, and sentenced to serve as slaves in the galleys. Some were even sentenced to death for the grave sin of heresy.

1751

Pope Benedict XIV (1740 - 1758)
Providas Romanorum

Approaching the mid-century mark of the 1700s, in the Kingdoms of Spain and Naples, there was a growing need to act more strongly against the threat and infiltration of Freemasons. The Papal bull of Pope Clement XII against Freemasonry was only thirteen years old. However, it was old enough for some to raise doubts about its validity because his successor had not affirmed it since he took office on August 17, 1740. Therefore, the Kings of Spain and Naples pressed upon Pope Benedict XIV to affirm *In Eminenti apostolatus specula* in some manner that would give them ecclesial backing to continue the work to suppress Freemasonry.

According to *Providas Romanorum*:

1. **His predecessor's condemnation against Freemasonry was** *"for always. . . .* **He forbade everyone and individual Christians (under penalty of excommunication to incur ipso facto without any declaration, from which no one could be absolved by others, except at the point of death, other than the Roman Pontiff pro tempore) of attempting or daring to enter such companies, propagate them or give them favor or shelter, hide them, register to them, to join or intervene, and more....**

Following this confirmation of *In Eminenti apostolatus specula*, Pope Benedict XIV then inserted the full text of his successor's Papal bull into his. Such a thing is ubiquitous within the history of Papal documents. However, the action served to leave no questions or doubts among the faithful that the condemnation against Freemasonry was not a mere expiring magisterial teaching of Pope Clement XII, but rather, that of Christ and His Church, always and forever.

In paragraph seven (7) of Providas Romanorum, Pope Benedict XIV affirms his predecessor's findings against Freemasonry. He moves to further elaborate upon those findings in six points:

> "In truth, among the very serious reasons of the aforementioned prohibitions and condemnations set forth in the aforementioned Constitution there is one, by virtue of which men of any religion and sect may unite with one another in such Societies and Conventicles; it is clear what harm can be done to the purity of the Catholic religion."

> "The second reason is the closed and impenetrable promise of secrecy, by virtue of which hides what is done in these meetings . . ."

> "The third reason is the oath with which they undertake to observe inviolably this secret, as if it were lawful for someone, questioned by legitimate power, with the excuse of some promise or oath to avoid the obligation to confess all that is sought, to know if in these Conventicles something contrary to the stability and the laws of the Religion and the

Republic is done."

"The fourth reason is that these societies oppose civil sanctions no less than the canons, bearing in mind, in fact, that in accordance with civil law all the colleges and meetings formed without public authority are forbidden. . . ."

"The fifth reason is that in many countries the aforementioned Societies and Aggregations have already been proscribed and banned with laws of Secular Princes."

"Finally, the last reason is that among the prudent and honest men the aforementioned Societies and Aggregations were blamed: in their judgment, anyone who enrolled in them was accused of blasphemy and perversion."

Providas Romanarum would be the final Papal document that explicitly and specifically addressed the error of Freemasonry until Pope Pius IX's *Etsi Multa* in 1873. Until then, there would be four documents that addressed the broader subject of secret societies (*Quo Graviora,* Pope Leo XII (1825), *Traditi Humiltati*, Pope Pius VIII (1829) and *Qui Pluribus*, Bl. Pope Pius IX (1846)), as others had cropped up around Europe and the Americas that were exercising similar philosophies and political agendas as Freemasonry, such as the Carbonari (*Ecclesiam a Jesu Christo*, Pope Pius VII (1821)). Three documents attacked the heresy of indifferentism, which is the first objection that Catholicism has with Freemasonry (*Mirari Vos*, Pope Gregory XVI (1832), *Inter Multiplices*, Bl. Pope

Pius IX (1853), and *Quanto Conficiamur Moerore*, Bl. Pope Pius IX (1863).

The critical instance of Pope Leo XII's (1823 – 1829) 1826 *Quo Graviora* followed a similar format to *Providas Romanorum* by including the text of *In Eminenti, Providas Romanorum, and Ecclesiam a Jesu Christo* to demonstrate that the prohibition against Freemasonry and the Carbonari is a permanent (dogmatic) teaching of the Church. It also invoked the wrath of Ss. Peter and Paul, as did *Providas Romanorum.* Distinct from the three previous documents, *Quo Gaviora* was issued from the Seat of Peter, together with all other factors included, qualifies it as having met the future criteria of being an infallible pronouncement of a Supreme Pontiff. Also distinct was the fact that *Quo Graviora* not only repeated the prohibition against Freemasonry and the Carbonari, but it also extended that same prohibition to all secret societies then present in 1826 and all those that will come in the future that rise up against the Catholic Church:

"Since matters are in such a state, We judge it to be the Character of our Office to Condemn these clandestine sects again, and in such a manner indeed that no one of them can boast that they are not encompassed by Our Apostolic Pronouncement, and under this pretext lead careless and less sagacious men into error. Therefore, from the Counsel of Our Venerable Brethren, the Cardinals of the Holy Roman Church, and also by Our own motion indeed with Our certain knowledge

and mature consideration, We forbid forever under the same penalties which are contained in the Letters of Our Predecessors already reported in this Our Constitution, which Letters We expressly confirm, that all secret societies, those which now are and those which perhaps will afterwards sprout out, and which propose to themselves against the Church and against the highest civil powers those things which We have mentioned above, by whatever name they may finally be called."

Despite the efforts of the Catholic Church to protect the faithful and to expose evil for what it is, the world would continue to witness Freemasonry spread to every country where Protestantism and indifferentism had been normalized.

1873

Bl. Pope Pius IX (1846 —1878)

Etsi Multa

Twenty-seven years after the beginning of his Papacy, Pope Pius IX promulgated *Etsi Multi,* in which he outlined all the dangers threatening the Catholic Church from within and without in Europe.

The primary issue being addressed in this encyclical is Kulturkampf (i.e., culture struggle), a sweeping series of anti-clerical reform laws in Germany, Switzerland, Austria, Italy, and Belgium. These news laws were primarily attempting to seize the state control of education out of the hands of the Catholic Church and to control ecclesial appointments. Pope Pius IX believed that Freemasons and the philosophy of Freemasonry were generally responsible for Kulturkampf.

Prior to paragraph number twenty-eight, where he explains the dangers of Freemasonry and how it is responsible for Kulturkampf, Pius IX addressed the events of recent persecutions against women "driven from their houses" in a hostile manner, the new anti-Catholic laws and religious persecution in Switzerland and Germany, the German endorsement of the Old Catholic Church ("openly support those recent heretics who call themselves Old Catholics"), the excommunication of Joseph Hubert Reinkens, who was elected Bishop of Germany for the Old Catholic Church.

In this challenging encyclical, Pope Pius IX draws from Scripture, the wealth of Church teaching, and pious writers, such as Saint Cyprian of Carthage, Saint Ambrose, Saint Augustine, Saint Peter Chrysologus, Saint Boniface, and Saint Leo the Great.

In paragraph twenty-eight (28), Blessed Pope Pius IX points to Masonic sects and other sects, whose intentions inveigh against the spiritual or temporal interests of the Catholic Church, as the source of why the war against the Church *"extends so widely."* He believes these borderless secret societies have exported and imported persecution against the Catholic Church. Pius IX says we can know if this is true by comparing what these groups profess with the *"nature, purpose, and amplitude of the conflict"* being waged. Through this comparison, Pius offers there can be no *"doubt but that the present calamity must be attributed to their deceits and machinations for the most part."*

Etsi Multa is the first instance of a Pope referring to Freemasonry and secret sects like them as a *"Synagogue of Satan,"* which makes its usage a striking escalation of the Church's understanding of the danger and threat that these groups pose to God's People. In the book of *Revelation* (vv. 2:9 and 3:9) and throughout the early tradition of pious Catholic writing, the term *"Synagogue of Satan"* was a term reserved exclusively for groups that teach heresy but pretend to be orthodox so that they can steal Christ's flock.

In paragraph twenty-nine of *Etsi Multa*, Bl. Pope Pius IX explains how the Church arrived at this position of being hated. It is due to the laxity and apathy of those under whose charge it is to enforce what the Church teaches, and that is why the Church is now being persecuted. Turning a blind eye to these synagogues of Satan has allowed them to achieve their goal of subjecting the Catholic Church *"to a most harsh servitude, to tear up the supports on which it rests, and to attempt to distort the marks by which it stands out gloriously."* If it were possible, though it is not, these groups would completely wipe out the Catholic Church *"from the world after they had shaken it with frequent blows, ruined it, and overturned it."*

Paragraph thirty (30) of *Etsi Multa* is crucial in the history of Papal pronouncements against Freemasonry because it not only charges bishops to apply all their efforts to protect those under their care against *"the snares and contagions of these sects"* and to bring back those who have *"unhappily joined,"* but it offers, most succinctly, the perfect roadmap on how to accomplish these things. According to Bl. Pope Pius IX, these are the three steps to prevent Catholics from falling into Freemasonry and how to bring those who have fallen into its error back in the faith:

To expose them to the error of thinking, Freemasonry is just an organization engaged in polite socializing, progressive civic engagement, charity work, or mutual benefits. We saw this, perhaps, with Haydn, whose petition for membership expressed that he thought Freemasonry was just a social organization. Today, Freemasons and appendant Masonic bodies like the Shriners aggressively push this idea out into the public that charity work is a central emphasis of their organization. Still today, people join Freemasonry due to this clever marketing scheme and pretentiousness.

To explain to them the dogmatic teaching on this matter that the Supreme Pontiffs have promulgated. Here, the holy Pontiff affirms that arguing that Catholics cannot be Freemasons based upon what Freemasonry teaches about itself is ineffective. The most effective method, according to Bl. Pope Pius IX, here, is to argue that Catholics cannot be Freemasons based upon what the Catholic Church teaches about Freemasonry and

To teach them that the prohibition against Freemasonry and sects like them is global; it is not just for Europe, but also for all continents *"and in other regions of the world."* This is a vital point because, in the coming decades and centuries, there will be efforts made by Catholics to argue that the Anglo and Prince Hall Masonic sects are acceptable for Catholics to join. This will cause the Catholic Church to revisit the topic and affirm, once again, that no matter the region where Freemasonry is being practiced, or the race of people practicing it, the principles of Freemasonry remain in them and, thereby, the Church makes no distinctions or gives dispensations for the various sects of Freemasonry.

The importance of *Etsi Multa* is that it was the first time in over a century that the prohibition against Freemasonry had been revisited as an individual topic and not part of the broader subject of secret societies or Masonic philosophes, such as indifferentism. By name, Bl. Pius IX cites how *Etsi Multa* belongs to the body of previous Papal pronouncements on this issue and states that the Catholic Church maintains the exact prohibitions against Freemasonry that his predecessors set forth.

Another essential statement included in *Etsi Multa* was the clarification (again) that the Catholic Church does not recognize any of the distinctions within Freemasonry and that the Catholic Church's prohibition against Freemasonry is global and not specific to just Europe. Also unique is the three-step action to prevent Catholics from falling into the error of Freemasonry and how to bring those who have fallen into its error back into the faith. Pope Leo XIII's encyclical Humanum Genus will include a similar action plan.

1884 — 1894

Pope Leo XIII (1878 — 1903)

Humanum Genus (1884)

Officio Sanctissimo (1887)

Dall'alto dell'Apostolicio Seggio (1890)

Custodi Di Quella Fede (1892)

Inimica Vis (1892)

Praeclara Gratulationis (1894)

From 1884 to 1894, over two decades, Pope Leo XIII promulgated five encyclicals and one apostolic exhortation on the dangers of Freemasonry and why the Catholic Church has dogmatically condemned and prohibited it. All of the papal issuances concerning Freemasonry, which followed his Humanum Genus, only further elaborated upon the arguments thereto. The only exception would be *Custoi Di Quella Fede*, which took time to outline the critical attacks that Freemasons have made against the Catholic Church in their war against us.

In this compendium chapter, we will consider Pope Leo XIII's unique contributions to the Catholic Church's dogmatic teaching against Freemasonry found in the two aforementioned encyclicals.

Humanum Genus (1884)

In paragraph six (6) of Humanum Genus, Pope Leo XIII affirms his predecessors and the Catholic Church's dogmatic teaching against Freemasonry, writing, *"**For as soon as the constitution and the spirit of the masonic sect were clearly discovered by manifest signs of its actions, by the investigation of its causes, by publication of its laws, and of its rites and commentaries, with the addition often of the personal testimony of those who were in the secret, this apostolic see denounced the sect of the**

Freemasons, and publicly declared its constitution, as contrary to law and right, to be pernicious no less to Christendom than to the State; and it forbade any one to enter the society, under the penalties which the Church is wont to inflict upon exceptionally guilty persons.

In paragraph eight (8) - the final preface to this complete treatment against Freemasonry, Pope Leo XIII returns to explaining why it belongs to his Apostolic duties as the Supreme Pontiff to *"arrest the contagion of this fatal plague."* He states that while in previous documents he attacked Masonic philosophy indirectly by demonstrating how it is related to other false teachings, such as socialism, communism, nihilism, and divorce, now here in Humanum Genus, he will offer a direct and frontal attack against Freemasonry and sects like it.

In paragraphs nine (9) and ten (10), Pope Leo XII affirms that this teaching against Freemasonry also applies to all Masonic sects, however associated. *"There are several organized bodies which, though differing in name, in ceremonial, in form and origin, are nevertheless so bound together by community of purpose and by the similarity of their main opinions, as to make in fact one thing with the sect of the Freemasons, which is a kind of center whence they all go forth, and whither they all return."*

He continues, ***"Candidates are generally commanded to promise - nay, with a special oath, to swear - that they will never, to any person, at any time or in any way, make known the members, the passes, or the subjects discussed. Thus, with a fraudulent external appearance, and with a style of simulation which is always the same, the Freemasons, like the Manichees of old, strive, as far as possible, to conceal themselves, and to admit no witnesses but their own members."***

Pope Leo XII understands that, on the one hand, Freemasonry attempts to create a public face through its publications, newspapers, love for people experiencing poverty, desire for cultural refinement, learning, and scholarship. On the other hand, the inner workings (invisible from public view) of Freemasonry are worthy of being compared to the pseudo-Christian and gnostic religion called Manichaeism from the third century. By selecting its own members and binding them to secrecy and obedience under pain of fatal penalties, Freemasonry can hide its deepest mysteries and designs from the public and its members of lower grades. Leo XIII calls this obligated promise to assassinate their members if they reveal their secrets a form of enslavement and contrary to natural virtue and uprightness.

Drawing from Matthew 7:18, Leo XIII finds that Freemasonry is corrupt with evil at its core, and no bad tree can produce bad fruit; thereby, *"the masonic sect produces fruits that are pernicious and of the bitterest savor."*

This section closes with Leo XIII stating that as a proof already provided, the true objective of Freemasonry is to supplant the Catholic Church by installing a new world order of religion and politics that is inspired by naturalism and which completely diverges from the divinely inspired order of religion and politics that has been brought and nurtured through Christian teaching.

In paragraph eleven (11), before Pope Leo XIII begins his treatise on the relationship between Freemasonry and naturalism, he moves this paragraph to define how he is using the term 'Freemasonry.' First, he states that using the term 'Freemasonry' is to encompass all of the appendant Masonic bodies broadly. Second, he admits that every person associated with Freemasonry, *"although not free from the guilt of having entangled themselves in such associations,"* may not be fully aware of the evil they are partaking. Similarly, it is the case with some of the appendant

Masonic bodies that may differ in some aspects from what is appropriately called 'Freemasonry' but are not entirely alien from what they have attached themselves. Therefore, they, too, can be judged according to the philosophy of their parent body.

In paragraphs 12 (twelve) to 19 (nineteen), Pope Leo XIII builds upon Pope Clement XII's teaching in *In Eminenti apostolatus specula* that Freemasonry practices naturalism. Then, he tied the practice of naturalism with the heresy of indifferentism, which also belonged to Clement XII's first theological argument against Freemasonry.

"Now, the fundamental doctrine of the naturalists, which they sufficiently make known by their very name, is that human nature and human reason ought in all things to be mistress and guide. Laying this down, they care little for duties to God, or pervert them by erroneous and vague opinions. For they deny that anything has been taught by God; they allow no dogma of religion or truth which cannot be understood by the human intelligence, nor any teacher who ought to be believed by reason of his authority."

Leo XIII's very generic working definition of naturalism is simply a philosophy that denies the intentional intercession of God through revelation, grace, and supernatural works; rather, it is through natural laws that things come to be what they are. That is, *"human nature and human reason ought be in all things to be mistress and guide."*

Freemasons are indeed taught that through his intellect and reason, he comes to know how to apply the liberal arts and sciences (e.g., rhetoric, logic, and geometry) and the working tools of an operative mason to his own life for the benefit of self-improvement.

As a naturalistic philosophy, Freemasonry promotes autonomy on several levels, such as freedom from authority and freedom from religious dogma by choosing how one's intellect and reason will guide them to build their own life, as long as it remains within the circumscribed bounds of Masonic law.

Freemasonry intends to build into its initiates a Masonic conscience, which, from the Catholic perspective, is a deformed conscience because it rejects divine revelation as the basis of its life. Denying supernatural faith and the efficacy of God's grace and relying only on reason, logic, and things that are perceptible to the senses, the Masonic conscience is the crowning height of naturalism par excellence.

Pope Leo XIII understood that the religious

naturalism found in Freemasonry inveighs against what he views as the two duties of the Catholic Church, which are to proclaim, defend, and teach the Gospel and to administer the sacraments (i.e., offer divine help to salvation).

The seed of indifferentism towards religion that Freemasonry has exported throughout the world ruins "all forms of religion," especially Catholicism, which posits that it proclaims with authority the fullness of truth. There is no reconciliation between Catholicism, which teaches that there is no religion equal to it because it proclaims the fullness of God's truth and the teaching of Freemasonry that Catholicism is just one of many mere opinions of man.

However, when indifferentism is married with naturalism, the fruit of Freemasonry wields something far graver. While the initiate first learns to subjugate the name of his personal God into a pantheistic collection of other gods, his advancement in learning how to apply the liberal arts and sciences and the working tools of an operative mason is teaching him that he does not need God at all. It is through this light of reason alone that either convinces the Freemason that there is no personal God interested in assisting him or that the existence of God needs to be questioned altogether.

Leo XII finds it a joke that Freemasons may profess the existence of God, but **"they themselves are witnesses that they do not all maintain this truth with the full assent of the mind or with a firm conviction."** How can they profess God's existence but simultaneously confess that God is not exceptional, all true and without equal? How can they profess the existence of God but simultaneously bind themselves to an organization in which they cannot discuss God or even mention the personal name of their God during open lodge meetings?

6. In paragraphs twenty (twenty) to 38 (thirty-eight), Pope Leo XIII narrates the relationship between naturalism and representative government and pushes back against the Masonic idea of 'separation of Church and State,' which has only led to the states thinking that they have a right to determine who is married according to civil contracts. Separation of Church and State has also opened the door for Freemasons to become intimately involved with the movement to secularize education; **"and in many places, they have procured that the education of youth shall be exclusively in the hands of laymen, and that nothing which treats of the most important and**

most holy duties of men to God shall be introduced into the instructions on morals." According to Leo XIII, society benefits when the state listens to the teaching authority of the Church on matters that affect the well-being of its citizens.

Having demonstrated that Freemasonry is using its chief dogma of naturalism to deconstruct the very foundations of society, in these paragraphs, Pope Leo XIII makes six succinct points about the mission and outcome of its effort:

Freemasonry wishes to replace Catholicism with the customs of paganism. "In this insane and wicked endeavor, we may almost see the implacable hatred and spirit of revenge with which Satan himself is inflamed against Jesus Christ." This endeavor of Freemasonry "tends only to the ignominious and disgraceful ruin of the human race."

Men were created for the society which Christ, through His Church, has inspired to be just and civil through the authority of His rule. In contrast, Freemasonry attempts to replace the rule of justice and civility with a society ruled by autonomy.

The teaching that all men are equal should not be determined to mean that they are autonomous and free to follow their own will. "If they are to be all equal, and each is to follow his own will, the

State will appear most deformed . . ." Men are equal in origin and nature. However, different in abilities, dignity, physical characteristics, disposition, and mannerisms, their common pursuit should not be individual happiness but a mutual conspiring for the common good, which will conform the state with the nature that God intended.

Through deliberate planning, Freemasons are working with socialists and communists to overthrow society's fear of God and reverence for divine laws and replace it with human worship. However, if their plots do not come to fruition, it is not because they have not committed to their effort; instead, it is because the divine religion cannot be destroyed and because men who refuse to be enslaved to secret societies "vigorously resist their insane attempts."

Freemasons have ingratiated themselves with rulers "under the pretense of friendship" and have convinced many that the Catholic Church is their enemy and a threat to their authority and sovereignty. Through this campaign of whispering into the ears of rulers, Freemasonry secured its security and began exercising significant influence in governments.

Freemasons have also deluded the masses by

charging that the Church and their ruler's relationship with the Church are why they are not as accessible and rich as they deserve. This campaign of whispering into the ears of the common people has "have urged them to assail both the Church and the civil power." Leo XIII believed that these attacks were an attack on the order that Divine Providence had instituted, and such rash attacks usually result in the penalty of their pride, which is more affliction and misery.

In response to the Masonic plot, Pope Leo XIII outlined the key tactics bishops, priests, and laypeople could implement to remedy the world of what he calls a **"fatal plague."**

1. Be conscientious and **"careful not in the least to depart from what the apostolic see has commanded in this matter."** That is, there is no allowance for those in the present or future to deviate from this dogmatic teaching against Freemasonry.

2. Bishops must make it their priority to uproot and destroy "this foul plague" through unremitting and persistent sermons and pastoral letters to instruct people about the sacred truths of the Church and also the clever strategies used by Freemasonry and societies like it to seduce unwitting men into

their ranks.

3. Bishops must engage the clergy and laity in this battle so that their love and knowledge of the Church will grow, and they will be less likely to fall into the snares of secret societies. In addition, the bishops should support and encourage the laity in seeking membership into the Third Order of Saint Francis and associations of guilds for workers like Saint Vincent's Society. Such Christian-oriented organizations can suppress interest in Freemasonry by giving men and women fraternity and the opportunity to labor for the common good and to be detached from the contagion of evil.

4. Bishops must devote the most significant part of their care to the instruction of the youth. They should keep them away from schools under the influence of Freemasonry and, under their guidance, let parents, religious teachers, and priests warn children about the danger and nature of Freemasonry so that they will not become ensnared.

5. Christians must join in prayer to beg for God's help. As Freemasons are united in secret councils and are bound to assist one another toward their evil ends, so too should

Christians "form the widest possible association of action and prayer." Christians must seek out the intercession of the Virgin Mary, Saint Michael, the prince of the Heavenly Angels, Saint Joseph, the spouse of the most holy Virgin and heavenly patron of the Catholic Church, and Ss. Peter and Paul are the fathers and victorious champions of the Christian faith. **"By their patronage, and by perseverance in united prayer, we hope that God will mercifully and opportunely succor the human race, which is encompassed by so many dangers."**

Due to its exhaustive precision, incisiveness, and prophetic content, Leo XIII's Humanum Genus is the most well-known and cited Papal document on Freemasonry. Its place in the Church as an encyclical teaching tool lies in its examination of Freemasonry as a naturalistic philosophy and its societal impacts.

Custodi Di Quella Fede (1892)

Following the political victory of Italy's Historical Right part in the 1892 General election, which he actively campaigned in, Pope Leo XIII seized upon the small victory to publish two encyclicals on the same day that repeated his similar themes. Whereas *Dall'alto dell'Apostolicio*

Seggio was written "To the Bishops, the Clergy, and the People of Italy," *Custodi Di Quella Fede* was addressed "To the Italian People." *Inimica Vis* was addressed "To the Bishops of Italy."

In the opening paragraphs of *Custodi Di Quella*, Pope Leo XII maintains that the Masonic sect is the chief source of this war against the Catholic Church and the historic Catholic culture of Italy, and states that in *Humanum Genus* and *Dall'alto dell'Apostolicio Seggio*, **"We tore from the face of masonry the mask which it used to hide itself and We showed it in its crude deformity and dark fatal activity."** In the former work, Leo XIII posited that naturalism is a core Masonic principle, which was an expansion of the Church's traditional position since Clement XII, that indifferentism was the core principle of Freemasonry. In the latter work, Leo XIII explained how the principles of Freemasonry had been exported worldwide to launch a war against the Catholic Church to supplant it as the source of truth.

In paragraphs 3 through 5, Leo XIII repeats his knowledge of the Masonic program's effort to convince people that Freemasonry is a philanthropic society interested in helping people. Nevertheless, all it has offered Italy is **"conspiracies, corruptions, and violence"** to dominate it. As for a litany of the evils that have overcome Italy in such a short period, Leo XIII presents:

1. The substitution of Christianity for naturalism.

2. Substituting the worship of faith with the worship of reason.

3. The substitution of Catholic morality for independent morality.

4. Substituting spiritual progress with material progress.

5. The seizing of Church property, money, and goods that have been squandered.

6. The substitution of holy maxims and laws from the Gospel with a code of revolution.

7. The insertion of atheistic doctrines and a vile realism in schools, science, and the Christian arts.

8. Reducing the number of priests by forcing an unnecessary number of clerics to serve in the military.

9. Substituting of the Sacrament of Holy Matrimony and the Funeral Mass with civil marriages and funerals.

10. An overall effort to laicize everything; thereby, replacing the role of the Church in society.

11. Attempting to silence and discredit the Catholic press.

12. Closed monasteries and convents but allowed Masonic lodges and sectarian dens to multiply.

13. Gave rights of association to all kinds of organizations but denied the same legal rights to religious societies.

14. Proclaimed freedom of religion but exercised intolerance towards Catholicism.

15. Promised the Pope's protection, dignity, and independence but exercised a daily contempt of him.

16. Allowances for public demonstrations against the Pope, but denied the same rights for Catholic demonstrations.

17. The encouragement of "schisms, apostasies, and revolts against legitimate superiors in the Church."

18. Allowed for oaths in impious associations, but vows made for religious obedience are rebuked for being "contrary to human dignity and freedom."

Following this itemization of the successes of the Masonic Program, in paragraph 6, Leo XIII notes that he does not want to create a Masonic bogeyman, as if Freemasons deserve all the credit for all the evil in the world. However, given the direct role that Freemasons have played in the revolutions, in Kulturkampf, and in infiltrating governments to press for the persecution of the Catholic Church, Leo XIII is confident that the spirit of Freemasonry has been the chief instigator of evil for the past thirty years. Leo XIII does not cite what source he is referring to when he writes, **"Proud of its successes, the sect herself has spoken out and told us all its past accomplishments and future goals."** However, there seems to have been either an article in a Masonic periodical or book or series of lectures where the triumphs and successes of the Masonic program had been exalted.

Then, in paragraphs 9—12 of *Custodi di Quella Fede*, Pope Leo XIII offers his most potent condemnation of Freemasonry by essentially calling it a sick joke. First, he returns to the point that he began making in *Humanum Genus* about how Freemasonry denies the supernatural because it relies solely on reason and logic – denying divine revelation – to fulfill its promise to improve the condition of man. **"Through its plans and works, it bases itself solely and entirely on such a weak and corrupt nature as ours. When these three concupiscences are brought to the extreme, the oppressions, greed, and seductive corruptions spread slowly. They take on boundless dimensions and become the oppression, plundering and source of corruption of an entire people."**

Next, Leo XIII flatly calls Freemasonry **"an enemy of God, Church, and country."** He charges everyone to see it for what it is and defend themselves from its pretensions, promises, seducements, enticements, and threats. Most clearly, the Supreme Pontiff charges that **"Christianity and masonry are essentially irreconcilable, such that to join one is to divorce the other,"** and that ignorance of this

41

incompatibility can no longer be ignored because "you have been warned openly by Our predecessors, and We have loudly repeated the warning."

Third, Leo XIII moves onto the consequences reserved for those who have fallen into **"one of these societies of perdition."** They are to separate themselves from it or remain separated from Christian communion. If they should choose the latter, they lose their soul now and for eternity. He then charges parents, teachers, godparents, and whoever has cared for other persons with the duty to use all prudence to protect those under their care from being seduced into joining these sects **"or to draw them from it if they have already entered."**

Fourth, he illustrates examples of what that care for the soul of others looks like. It means **"should fear the least danger, avoid every occasion, and take the greatest precautions,"** using **"all the prudence of the serpent, while keeping in your heart the simplicity of the dove,"** fathers and mothers being cautious of inviting strangers into their homes, especially before their visitor's faith life have sufficiently determined, and to be aware of what friends, teachers, doctors, or other benefactors, are recruiters for these guilty sects. In closing, Leo XIII laments how Freemasons have infiltrated families, penetrating them as wolves in sheep's clothing.

The 20th Century

After 169 years of consistent Papal teachings on the prohibition against Freemasonry and its appendant bodies, Pope Pius X would be the last Pope to address the issue in the form of a Papal Bull, Encyclical, or Apostolic Exhortation. In his 1907 *Une Fois Encore* (Once Again), Pius X responded to this false claim that the Vatican was attempting to instigate a religious war in France by pointing to Freemasonry and other groups as being the true instigators of a war against the Catholic Church:

The Church, they said, is seeking to arouse religious war in France and is summoning to her aid the violent persecution which has been the object of her prayers. What a strange accusation! Founded by Him who came to bring peace to the world and to reconcile man with God, a Messenger of peace upon earth, the Church could only seek religious war by repudiating her high mission and belying it before the eyes of all. To this mission of patient sweetness and love she rests and will remain always faithful. Besides, the whole world now knows that if peace of conscience is broken in France, that is not the work of the Church but of her enemies. Fair-minded men, even though not of our faith, recognize that if there is a struggle on the question of religion in your beloved country, it is not because the Church was the first to unfurl the flag, but because war was declared against her. During the last twenty-five years she has had to undergo this warfare.

That is the truth and the proof of it is seen in the declarations made and repeated over and over again in the Press, at meetings, at Masonic congresses, and even in Parliament, as well as in the attacks which have been progressively and systematically directed against her. These facts are undeniable, and no argument can ever make away with them. The Church then does not wish for war and religious war least of all. To affirm the contrary is an outrageous calumny.

After 169 years of consistent Papal teachings on the prohibition against Freemasonry and its appendant bodies, Pope Pius X would be the last Pope to address the issue in the form of a Papal Bull, Encyclical, or Apostolic Exhortation. In his 1907 *Une Fois Encore* (Once Again), Pius X responded to this false claim that the Vatican was attempting to instigate a religious war in France by pointing to Freemasonry and other groups as being the true instigators of a war against the Catholic Church:

The Church, they said, is seeking to arouse religious war in France and is summoning to her aid the violent persecution which has been the object of her prayers. What a strange accusation! Founded by Him who came to bring peace to the world and to reconcile man with God, a Messenger of peace upon earth, the Church could only seek religious war by repudiating her high mission and belying it before the eyes of all. To this mission of patient sweetness and love she rests and will remain always faithful. Besides, the whole world now knows that if peace of conscience is broken in France, that is not the work of the Church but of her enemies. Fair-minded men, even though not of our faith, recognize that if there is a struggle on the question of religion in your beloved country, it is not because the Church was the first to unfurl the flag, but because war was declared against her. During the last twenty-five years she has had to undergo this warfare. That is the truth and the proof of it is seen in the declarations made and repeated over and over again in the Press, at meetings, at Masonic congresses, and even in Parliament, as well as in the attacks which have been progressively and systematically directed against her. These facts are undeniable, and no argument can ever make away with them. The Church then does not wish for war and religious war least of all. To affirm the contrary is an outrageous calumny.

From this point forward, the previous prohibitions and penalties would be codified in the Church's Canon Law. This first official comprehensive codification of Canon Law was completed on May 27, 1917, and promulgated in the following year by Pope Benedict XV, thus earning it the name, 'the Pio-Benedictine Code.'

It was also in 1917, while the young Maximillian Kolbe was studying in Rome when he witnessed the Freemasons loudly celebrating their second centenary anniversary by demonstrating in the streets with black banners depicting the Archangel Saint Michael being trodden underfoot by Satan and people flaunting Masonic insignia beneath Vatican windows; some of which carried the words, *"Satan will rule on Vatican Hill, and the Pope will serve as his errand boy."* On that day, the future saint fulfilled his promise to the Virgin Mary to fight for her – he established the Knights of the Immaculata.

Canon No. 2335 (1917)

In 1917 Code of Canon Law, Canon No. 2335 was written to be a simple and very concise summation of the prohibitions against Freemasonry first promulgated by Pope Clement XII in his 1738 *In Eminenti*:

> (1917) CANON No. 2335: Persons joining associations of the Masonic sect or any others of the same kind which plot against the Church and legitimate civil authorities contract excommunication reserved to the Apostolic See.

The phrase therein contained, "plot against the Church and legitimate civil authorities . . ." is explained in paragraph (1) of In Eminenti as well as throughout *Etsi Multa, Humanum Genus, Officio Sanctissimo,* and *Dell'alto dell'Apostolico Seggio*. These Papal documents clearly explain that the plot of Freemasonry concerns the exportation of its ideologies of indifferentism, secularism, relativism, and naturalism, as well as its role in infiltrating and seducing governments in an attempt to stir revolutions as a means to supplant the authority, role, mission the Catholic Church in the world. Therefore, being well-grounded in the previous Papal encyclicals and apostolic exhortations, Canon No. 2335 is not an innovation but is in continuity with Church dogma and tradition, although weaker, because it only penalizes membership. Canon No. 2335 departs from the discipline of excommunicating those who assist with the Masonic plot and those who ally with Freemasons. The 1983 Canon will restore the former.

Canon No. 1374 (1983)

In the new Canon Law No. 1374, the word 'Masonic' was removed from the original phrase, "Persons joining associations of the Masonic sect or any others of the same kind which plot against the Church and legitimate civil authorities," to now state, "A person who joins an association which plots against the Church." In addition, the new Canon modified the penalty from "contract excommunication simply reserved to the Apostolic See" to state "[a person who joins] to be punished with a just penalty; however, a person who promotes or directs an association of this kind is to be punished with an interdict."

(1983) CANON No. 1374: A person who joins an association that plots against the Church is to be punished with a just penalty; however, a person who promotes or directs an association of this kind will be punished with an interdict.

The Code of Canons of Oriental Churches (CCEO), which was codified in 1990 for the twenty-three Eastern Catholic Churches that are union with the Seat of Peter, has a parallel canon to Canon No. 1374 of the 1983 Code of Canon Law for the Latins:

(1990) CCEO CANON No. 1448: 1. One who uses a public performance or talk or publicly disseminated writing, or other media of communication, to blaspheme, seriously harm good morals, injure religion or the Church, or incite hatred or contempt for religion or the Church, is to be punished with an appropriate penalty. 2. One who joins an organization which plots against the Church, is to be punished with an appropriate penalty.

The 1983 Code of Canon Law, also called the Johanno-Pauline Code, was promulgated by Pope John Paul II on January 25, 1983. The immediate reaction to Canon No. 1374 that year was that its new wording broadened the span of associations that plot against the Church beyond just being the Masonic sects to include such groups as communists and others, but that the determination of which associations Catholics could not belong to was left to the purview of individual bishops. It had seemed that the Masonic lobby of the Catholic Church had won the message despite the compromise.

Then, on November 26, 1983, just one day before the new Code of Canon Law was scheduled to take effect on the First Sunday of Advent, the Congregation of the Doctrine of Faith, under the leadership of Joseph Cardinal Ratzinger, published a Declaration on Masonic Associations, which Pope John Paul II approved.

Quaesitum Est (Query)
Congregation of the
Doctrine of the Faith (1983)

Declaration on Masonic Associations:

It has been asked whether there has been any change in the Church's decision regarding Masonic associations since the new Code of Canon Law does not mention them expressly, unlike the previous Code.

This Sacred Congregation is in a position to reply that this circumstance is due to an editorial criterion followed in the case of other unmentioned associations since they are contained in broader categories.

Therefore, the Church's negative judgment regarding Masonic association remains unchanged since their principles have always been considered irreconcilable with the doctrine of the Church. Therefore, membership in them remains forbidden. The faithful who enroll in

Masonic associations are in grave sin and may not receive Holy Communion.

It is not within the competence of local ecclesiastical authorities to give a judgment on the nature of Masonic associations, which would imply a derogation from what has been decided above, and this is in line with the Declaration of this Sacred Congregation issued on February 17, 1981 (cf. AAS 73 1981 pp. 240-241; English language edition of L'Osservatore Romano, March 9, 1981).

In an audience granted to the undersigned Cardinal Prefect, the Holy Pontiff John Paul II approved and ordered the publication of this Declaration, which had been decided in an ordinary meeting of this Sacred Congregation.

Rome, from the Office of the Sacred Congregation for the Doctrine of the Faith, November 26, 1983.

Joseph Card. RATZINGER

Prefect

+ Fr. Jerome Hamer, O.P.

Titular Archbishop of Lorium

Secretary

Ratzinger's Quaesitum Est is important because it

connects the general qualifier "an association which plots against the Church" with the specific Masonic qualifier "Masonic association remains unchanged since they always been considered irreconcilable with the doctrine of the Church . . ." By the term "principles," Ratzinger is bringing his Declaration into continuity with the preexisting dogmatic prohibition against Freemasonry, which has consistently defined the Masonic principles as indifferentism, relativism, secularism, and naturalism. Moreover, this declaration firmly states that it can never be under the purview of individual bishops to deviate from Church teaching and issue independent judgments "on the nature of Masonic associations."

Quaesitum Est is also important because it maintains that excommunication is the penalty reserved for those who join Masonic sects. Ratzinger states that the only reason the word 'Masonic' was not explicitly used in the new Code of Canon Law was "an editorial criterion." Inasmuch as we might speculate about the intentions of those who lobbied for such an editorial criterion, we cannot speculate whether the penalty has changed.

On the contrary, Quaesitum Est clearly states in three instances that excommunication is still the penalty reserved for those who join Masonic sects. First, Ratzinger states, **"the Church's negative judgment regarding Masonic association remains unchanged."** Unchanged, meaning that the 1983 Canon No. 1374 persists in continuity with the 1917 Canon No. 2335 and with every previous Papal Bull and encyclical on this issue. Second, he states that enrolling in Masonic associations is a "grave sin." Grave sin, according to Church teaching, "deprives us of communion with God and therefore makes up incapable of eternal life . . ."[1] Third, he states that those who enroll in Masonic associations "may not receive Holy Communion." Again, without stating the word 'excommunication,' Ratzinger has, in these three instances, pointed to excommunication as still being the penalty reserved for enrolling in Masonic sects. In this way, Quaesitum Est is in line with the Church's teaching on excommunication:

> Catechism of the Catholic Church Para. 1463 Certain particularly grave sins incur excommunication, the most severe ecclesiastical penalty, which impedes the reception of the sacraments and the exercise of certain ecclesiastical acts, and for which absolution consequently cannot be granted, according to canon law, except by the Pope, the bishop of the place or priests authorized by them.[2] In danger of death, even if deprived of faculties for hearing confessions, any priest can be absolved from every sin and excommunication.[3]

---

[1] Catechism of the Catholic Church, paragraph 1472. (2013 printing).

[2] Cf. ⇒ CIC, cann. 1331; ⇒ 1354-1357; CCEO, can. 1431; 1434; 1420.

[3] Cf. ⇒ CIC, can. 976; CCEO, can. 725.

In the instant case, excommunication for enrolling in Masonic sects is proven by Quaesitum Est, affirming it is a 'grave sin' and that it impedes the reception of the Sacrament of the Holy Eucharist (communion). Per Canon Law (1364 – 1399), the remedy for the penalty incurred for enrolling in Masonic associations is no longer reserved to the Pope alone but can now be resolved by a priest (with the proper faculties) through the Sacrament of Penance and Reconciliation, such as other grave sins can also be (e.g., murder, theft, masturbation, and adultery).

Other Resources on Freemasonry at SaintDominicsMedia.COM

The Catholic Catechism on Freemasonry: A Theological and Historical Treatment on the Catholic Church's Prohibition Against Freemasonry and its Appendant Masonic Bodies

This book contextualizes the history and provides a theological analysis and commentary on the nine Papal documents, two Canon Laws, and two documents issued by the Congregation of the Doctrine of the Faith, which relate specifically to the Catholic Church's dogmatic prohibition against Freemasonry.

MASTER CLASS: The Catholic Catechism on Freemasonry: A Lecture Series on Freemasonry Through the Light of Catholicism

This course will explore the historical and philosophical foundations of Freemasonry, as well as its relationship with religion and the Catholic Church. You will learn about the meaning and symbolism of the three degrees of Freemasonry: Entered Apprentice, Fellow Craft, and Master Mason. You will also examine the various documents issued by the popes and the Congregation for the Doctrine of the Faith that condemn Freemasonry and its teachings. Finally, you will analyze how Freemasonry fits into the current global scenario of the great reset or the reordering of the world.

Saint Dominic's Media

Founded in 2017, Saint Dominic's Media is a publisher of Catholic print, video, and other media. Our mission is to crusade for peace through truth by sharing and reflecting the Dominican spirit of a life devoted to liturgical prayer, the study of sacred truth, and zeal for the Catholic community.

David L. Gray is a 2006 covert to the Catholic Church, David L. Gray (born 1972) is an American Catholic Theologian, Historian, and Humorist. He is also the founding President and Publisher of Saint Dominic's Media. David L. Gray holds a Bachelor of Science in Business Administration from Central State University (Ohio) and a Master of Arts in Catholic Theology from Ohio Dominican University.

His anthology of Catholic books includes *Dead on Arrival: The Seven Fatal Errors of Sola Scriptura, Cooperating with God: The Bridegroom's Prayer, Cooperating with God: Life with Cross, The Divine Symphony: An Exordium on the Theology of the Catholic Mass, The Catholic Catechism on Freemasonry: A Theological and Historical Treatment on the Catholic Church's Prohibition Against Freemasonry and Its Appendant Masonic Bodies*, and *Catholic, Traditional & Black: In Anthology and Discourse*.

Once a prominent Masonic leader, author, and speaker, David L. Gray had reached some of the highest ranks and honors in the Masonic order. However, upon entering the Catholic Church, he left Freemasonry, becoming a passionate defender of the Catholic Church's dogmatic teaching against Freemasonry. He is now a well-known Catholic speaker, writer, and media producer. You can find out more about him at davidlgray.info and saintdominicsmedia.com